W9-CAZ-297

Life in an
Anishinabe Camp

Niki Walker

Crabtree Publishing Company

www.crabtreebooks.com

Life in an Anishinabe Camp

Created by Bobbie Kalman

Dedicated by Niki Walker
To Don and Melissa

Editor-in-Chief
Bobbie Kalman

Author and Editorial director
Niki Walker

Editors
Kathryn Smithyman
Amanda Bishop

Copy editors
Molly Aloian
Rebecca Sjonger

Researcher
Deanna Brady

Art director
Robert MacGregor

Design
Margaret Amy Reiach

Production coordinator
Heather Fitzpatrick

Photo research
Laura Hysert
Jaimie Nathan

Consultants
Dr. Jon Parmenter, Assistant Professor, Department of History
   Coordinator, Native American Studies Program, St. Lawrence University
Professor Leanne Simpson, Ph.D., Director, Indigenous Environmental
   Studies, Department of Native Studies, Trent University

Photographs and reproductions
American Museum of Natural History Library: page 14
Beloit College, Logan Museum of Anthropology: page 21
Lois Beardslee, reprinted courtesy of Traverse Area District Library,
   Traverse City, MI: pages 28-29
Bill Lindner Photography: page 31
Frances Anne Hopkins/National Archives of Canada/Copy negative
   number C-002771: page 30
© Permission of Lazare & Parker: front cover, pages 15, 17, 20, 22
With Permission of the Royal Ontario Museum © ROM: page 6
The University of Michigan Exhibit Museum of Natural History:
   title page, pages 5, 8, 10
Eastman Johnson Collection, acc. #62.181.1, St. Louis County
   Historical Society: back cover

Illustrations
Barbara Bedell: pages 6, 15, 23, 27
Katherine Kantor: pages 4 (top), 9 (bottom), 16 (top), 18 (top left),
   19 (top), 26
Margaret Amy Reiach: border, pages 7, 8, 9 (top), 11, 12-13, 16 (bottom),
   18 (top right, bottom), 19 (middle, bottom), 20, 21, 22, 24, 25, 29,
   back cover (hide background)
Bonna Rouse: background (title page, pages 2, 3), page 4 (bottom)

Crabtree Publishing Company

www.crabtreebooks.com   1-800-387-7650

PMB 16A	612 Welland Avenue	73 Lime Walk
350 Fifth Avenue	St. Catharines	Headington
Suite 3308	Ontario	Oxford
New York, NY	Canada	OX3 7AD
10118	L2M 5V6	United Kingdom

Cataloging-in-Publication Data
Walker, Niki
   Life in an Anishinabe camp/Niki Walker.
      p. cm. -- (Native nations of North America series)
Includes index.
This book introduces children to the daily life, customs, and
culture of the Anishinabe people in the western Great Lakes
region.
   ISBN 0-7787-0373-8 (RLB) -- ISBN 0-7787-0465-3 (pbk.)
1. Ojibwa Indians--Juvenile literature. [1. Ojibwa Indians.
2. Indians of North America--Great Lakes.] I. Title. II. Series.
E99.C6 K35 2003
977.004'973--dc21
                                                    LC 2002012052

Contents

Anishinabe

LAKE SUPERIOR

Anishinabe

Anishinabe

LAKE HURON

LAKE MICHIGAN

LAKE ONTARIO

LAKE ERIE

People of the lakes

Indigenous, or Native, peoples have lived in the Great Lakes region for thousands of years. The area was once covered in thick woodlands that included elm, birch, maple, and various coniferous trees. The forests were home to many animals, including deer, moose, elk, beaver, wolves, bears, and rabbits. The animals, plants, and fresh water of the lakes provided people with everything they needed.

People of the Anishinabe (Anishinaabe) **nation** lived in **territories** in the western Great Lakes region, as shown on the map above. The name "Anishinabe" means "the people" in their language, *Anishinabemowin* (*Nishnaabemwin*), which is an **Algonquian** language. The Anishinabe are also known as Ojibwe, Ojibwa, Ojibway, and Chippewa. These names were given to them by others.

Following the *megis*

According to **oral tradition**, the Anishinabe people once lived by a huge body of salt water, which may have been the Atlantic Ocean or Hudson's Bay. The people received a **prophecy**, or prediction, that if they traveled inland, they would find a place where food grew on water. Some went west, following a **vision** of a *megis*, or cowrie shell, that guided them to the western Great Lakes. There, they saw a type of grass called **wild rice**, which seemed to grow on the water. The people split into groups and settled in different spots. Together, they made up the Anishinabe nation.

The Three Fires

The Anishinabe had an especially close relationship with two other nations in the western Great Lakes region—the Odawa (Ottawa) and Potawatomi. People of these three nations often married one another, traded goods, and worked together to settle disputes. They also gathered at **councils**, where they made decisions together. Their **alliance**, known as "The Three Fires," was so close that people described it in family terms. The Anishinabe nation was considered the eldest brother; the Potawatomi nation was the youngest brother; and the Odawa nation was in the middle.

Families, clans, and councils

The Anishinabe nation was divided into many large groups, which were made up of several **extended families**. Extended families included grandparents, parents, children, aunts, uncles, and cousins. Most groups had between 300 and 400 people. The families in a group shared a large territory, but they lived together only part of the year—usually in big summer **camps**. The rest of the year, they lived in smaller camps made up of one or two families. People maintained ties with their groups year-round, however, with visits to one another's camps.

bear

Besides being part of a family of blood relatives, people also belonged to **clans** or **dodems**. There were five original Anishinabe dodems—marten, loon, crane, bear, and sturgeon. Members of each dodem were said to share the same **ancestor**, which was the spirit of the animal for which their dodem was named. Each animal had qualities that its clan members were said to have. Bears, for instance, were brave warriors, whereas cranes were good speakers. Dodem members often lived in different camps and even belonged to different nations. When people visited other camps, they looked for members of their dodem, who would offer them food and a place to stay.

marten

Councils

When the families in a territory had to make decisions that affected everyone, such as when to move or how to deal with neighboring nations, each clan sent representatives to a council. Most councils were held in summer, when families came together to camp. The clans did not always send the same representatives to councils. They sent the people who could best solve the problem being discussed. For instance, for decisions about hunting, the clans usually sent their best hunters as well as their spiritual leaders.

The representatives made decisions by **consensus**, which means they discussed issues and possible solutions until almost everyone agreed on the actions that they should take. No person had authority over others, and no one's interests were considered more important than those of the group as a whole. All members of a group were seen as equally important, but some people earned great respect for their wisdom, spiritual power, healing skills, or their ability to provide for their families.

sturgeon

Marriage and family ties

All members of a dodem were thought of as "brothers" and "sisters," whether they were blood relatives or not. People were not allowed to marry other members of their dodem. Young women were considered old enough to marry around the age of fifteen. Men usually married around the age of nineteen or twenty. There was no wedding ceremony. A couple lived together for a year and were then considered married. The couple spent the first year of their marriage living with the bride's parents. They worked together to gather and make everything they would need to set up their own home. If the couple had children, the children were part of the father's dodem.

crane

loon

Moving with the seasons

The Anishinabe based their lives on the four seasons of the Great Lakes region: winter, spring, summer, and autumn. Each season provided different plants and animals for the Anishinabe to use. When seasons changed, people moved their camps to the places within their territories where they would find the most food and natural materials for making clothing, tools, and shelters.

Winter tasks and tales

During the harsh winters, men spent the days hunting and ice fishing, while women and children usually stayed indoors, making clothing and household items. In the evenings, men made and repaired tools and weapons. During this time, the family **elders** told stories.

Spring jobs

The southern parts of the Anishinabe territories had forests of maple trees. In spring, families in these areas moved to the maple forests (above). They collected sap and boiled it down into syrup and sugar. Spring was also a time for cutting and peeling birch bark, which was used to make containers (above right), shelters, and **canoes**. Canoes are long and narrow lightweight boats.

Summer villages

In summer, huge groups of extended families camped together. They often returned to the same site year after year. Men spent their days fishing, hunting, and building new canoes. Women dried extra meat and fish and gathered foods such as berries from the forest. Most also planted vegetable gardens. Summer was also a time for the community to hold councils, ceremonies, and celebrations.

The fall gathering season

In early autumn, wild rice became ripe. People moved from their large summer camps to the marshy areas where the rice grew. Each family had its own spot for harvesting wild rice. Family members worked together to gather, dry, and store as much rice as they could before heading to their winter camps.

Name all the ways people in this picture are working with food. Find five other activities taking place at this Anishinabe summer village.

Setting up camp

Most Anishinabe traveled to different areas of their territories each season, but they usually returned to the same campsites year after year. They set up their camps for specific purposes, such as fishing, hunting, preparing maple sugar and wild rice, and holding special meetings and ceremonies. Summer camps were large. Winter hunting camps were much smaller—often just one or two families. Food was scarce in winter, and animals such as elk, deer, and moose traveled over huge areas. Families moved frequently to follow the animals, and it was easier to move a small group than a large one.

Since the Anishinabe moved each season, their housing had to be easy to carry and set up. For most of the year, they lived in **wigwams**. Wigwams had frames of wooden poles covered with birch bark or animal hides. When families moved from a campsite, they left the frames in place. They took their wigwam coverings with them, so they would not have to make new coverings each time they moved. People simply re-covered the frames when they returned the following year.

*On hunting trips, people often camped in **tipis**, which the Anishinabe called **bajiishka'ogaan**.*

Building a wigwam

Most wigwams were dome-shaped, although some looked like cones. They usually had round bases about ten feet (3 m) across. The largest wigwams were oval or rectangular, and they were up to thirty feet (9 m) in length. Most wigwams could be set up in less than a day. People usually set them up on a slight slope, so that rain would drain away from them. Families arranged their wigwams with the doorways facing east— the direction of the rising sun.

1. A wigwam's curved frame was made up of soft, young saplings. After removing the sapling's branches, men sunk the poles into holes in the ground to make the frame secure.

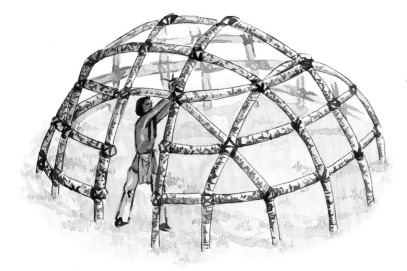

2. Next, the builders pulled down the tops of the saplings and tied them together with strips of animal hide or fibers of basswood bark to form the domed frame. They then lashed a few poles around the sides to make the frame sturdier.

3. Women covered the frame with sheets of birch bark or animal hides. They left a space for a doorway and hung an animal hide over it. A branch was stitched to the bottom of this hide to help weigh it down.

In the wigwam

Although many activities took place outdoors, wigwams were the center of family life, especially in colder weather. Families spent chilly evenings inside their wigwams, where they cooked, mended tools, sang songs, and told stories. Wigwams were usually shared by several **generations** of the same family.

Making things comfortable

People covered the ground inside the wigwam with mats made of woven rushes or cedar bark. For sleeping, they laid their bedding of soft, furry animal hides over the mats. During the day, they took the bedding outside and spread it over the wigwam to air it out.

Warm and cozy

A fireplace in the center of the wigwam heated the home. People also used it for cooking when the weather outside was cold or rainy. Smoke escaped through a hole in the top of the wigwam.

Tending the fire

At least one person stayed awake while the others were sleeping to keep an eye on the fire. The watcher made sure that sparks did not set the mats or bedding on fire. He or she used a wooden paddle to shove loose coals or smoldering grasses back into the fireplace.

Wigwams were cozy, even in cold weather. Families hung furs, mats, and extra sheets of birch bark around the insides of their wigwams to help keep out cold winds. On winter evenings, family members gathered inside their homes and enjoyed hearing the elders sing songs and tell stories.

Storage

People stored belongings in birchbark or cedar containers, such as the one on the left, which they propped against walls or hung from the frame. They stored extra food, wood, and clothing in **lean-tos**, right, or in holes in the ground, which they lined with birch bark.

Sharing the work

Living in the woodlands took skill, knowledge, planning, and hard work. Everyone in a camp worked together to make sure there was enough food as well as materials for shelter and clothing. Even small children helped as much as they could. Some jobs were traditionally performed by women and others by men. Men's jobs included hunting, which required strength, and trading, which involved traveling far from camp.

Men also made their own weapons and tools. Women were responsible for tasks such as gathering berries, seeds, and plants; cooking and **preserving** foods; weaving mats from rushes and other plants; and making and decorating clothing, bedding, and storage containers. They often helped with the hunting and fishing as well. Although men and women did different jobs, their work was considered equally important.

Protecting the camp

Some young men acted as **scouts**. They kept a watch for animals or strangers that wandered near the campsite or on the trails used by members of the camp. Scouts warned the people at the camp when something or someone was approaching. When moving camp, scouts often went ahead to check the new campsite.

Preparing food

Women cooked one main meal each day, which was usually eaten in the afternoon. They cooked soups and stews in containers made of birch bark. They did not hang the containers over a fire but, instead, dropped heated rocks into them to cook the foods. Along with soup or stew, women also served fruits, vegetables, or wild rice. Dried or smoked meat and fish and roasted corn were also popular foods. Women seasoned many meals with herbs or maple sugar.

Trading for goods

Some nations had artwork, crafts, foods, or materials that others nations did not have. People from different camps and nations often traded in order to obtain such goods. Trade goods included items made of copper; foods such as corn, maple sugar, and wild rice; weapons; birchbark containers and canoes; decorated items; and other useful or beautiful things. Trading was handled by men, who traveled to other camps or special meeting places with their canoes loaded. The goods that they traded were often made by women.

Women preserved meat by smoking it over a fire.

The Anishinabe traded with one another as well as with people from other nations.

Children's lives

Most Anishinabe families were small, having only two or three children. Parents saw their children as a gift, so they treated them with a great deal of respect and affection.

Close to mom

Mothers bundled their babies on **cradleboards** and carried them everywhere they went. They often strapped the cradleboards to their backs, like knapsacks. While they worked, mothers propped their cradleboards against trees or hung them from branches so that their babies could sleep or watch them work. Infants were bundled on the boards until they were about a year old. Their mothers unwrapped them several times a day to allow the babies to stretch.

Their place in the world

Grandparents spent a great deal of time teaching children about spirituality and their place in the world (see pages 28-29). Through the elders' songs and stories, children learned about the creation of the world, the Creator, various spirits, or **manitous**, and the history and culture of their people. Children learned that they were connected to all things and that they must respect the balance of nature.

Cradleboards were warm and snug.
A layer of moss between the baby and the hide acted as a diaper and kept the baby dry.

Women taught their daughters the art of biting designs into birch bark. Making bitten-bark artwork was a favorite winter pastime.

Education

Children spent their first seven years among the women and elders of the camp, learning values and life skills. They learned to share willingly and never to take more than they needed. When they were seven years old, children began learning the skills they would need as adults. They learned by watching and helping their parents. Girls spent time with their mothers, as well as their aunts and female cousins, who taught them how to prepare and preserve foods, treat hides, sew and decorate clothing, and make birchbark items. Fathers, uncles, and male cousins showed boys how to hunt, fish, and make tools, weapons, and canoes.

Passing into adulthood

Between the ages of ten and fourteen, a boy marked the end of his childhood with a **vision quest** (shown above). He went into the forest, where he **fasted** and stayed awake for days until he had a vision. The vision revealed his guardian manitou, who would guide and protect him. The boy also received guidance on which path he should follow in life. A girl marked the end of her childhood with a type of fast called a **berry fast**. She stopped eating berries for one year. During that time, she met each month with older women in her family and learned about the sacred role that she would one day have as a mother.

Materials from nature

Everything the Anishinabe had came from nature. They knew which materials were available in the lakes, fields, and forests each season and how they could best use these resources. People used hides, bones, teeth, **sinews**, claws, stones, shells, bark, and plant fibers to make the things they needed.

Animal hides

Animal hides could be made into clothing, shoes, bedding, and wigwam coverings.

Women skinned the animals men hunted and then prepared the hides for use by **tanning** them. Tanning made the hides very soft. It involved several steps and took many hours of hard work. Women used sharp bones or rocks to scrape the hides clean of meat, fat, and fur. They then soaked the hides in a liquid they made from the bark, acorns, and leaves of oak trees. This mixture contained a type of acid that preserved the hides and kept them soft, even after they were stretched and dried, as shown below. Women hung the hides used for clothing over wood fires. The hides absorbed the smell of smoke, which kept bugs away.

Rawhide
When animal hides were not tanned and stretched, they dried out and became very tough. This type of hard hide, called **rawhide**, was used to make items such as snowshoes, which had to be durable.

Snowshoes were essential for winter travel. They allowed people to walk over deep snow without sinking into it. Snowshoes were usually made of rawhide strips that were woven over wooden frames.

Plant fibers

In summer, women gathered rushes, reeds, and plant fibers and made them into many useful items, such as rope, bags, and mats. Sometimes women soaked the plants in natural dyes first, so that the finished items would have colorful designs and patterns. The patterns included diamonds, stripes, or crisscrosses.

Women wove mats on large wooden frames.

Birch bark

Birch bark was a very important material to the Anishinabe. They used it to make **scrolls** (see page 29), cover wigwams, and construct containers for collecting sap, storing foods, and cooking. One of the most essential items people made from this material was the birchbark canoe. The Anishinabe used canoes to travel the waterways almost year-round, except when the waters froze in winter. Their canoes had frames of cedar poles, which they covered with sheets of birch bark. The canoes were sealed with **pitch**, a type of natural glue that made them watertight.

*To make birchbark containers, women cut pieces of bark and punched holes along their edges with short, sharply pointed tools called **awls**. They threaded either sinew or plant fibers through the holes to stitch the pieces together.*

*In winter, the Anishinabe used **toboggans** to move goods and people from place to place. Toboggans were made of wood, hides, and rawhide. Some people had dogs to pull these sleds.*

Hunting and fishing

Spiritual leaders often advised hunters on where to hunt. The hunters then tracked the animals by looking for signs such as droppings or tracks in the snow.

Hunting and fishing provided the Anishinabe with many of the things they needed to survive. Hunting was not an easy task. Men had to know where animals could be found each season and how different animals behaved, especially when threatened. Hunters often traveled far from their camps in order to find animals. Sometimes they helped one another by working in small groups to herd the animals closer to the camps or to hunt large animals such as moose.

Winter survival

Men hunted and fished year-round, but these tasks became especially important in winter, when their families survived on stored foods and whatever the hunters could catch. In early winter, men caught beavers, ducks, and geese. The rest of the winter, they hunted moose, bears, elks, foxes, minks, and rabbits. They hunted deer year-round. A hunter never hunted his dodem animal!

20

Ways of hunting

Hunters used several methods to catch animals. They caught small animals, such as rabbits and foxes, in traps and **snares** and set up **deadfalls** to catch larger animals such as bears. A deadfall was a trap that was rigged to drop a heavy weight, such as a log, onto an animal that wandered into the trap. Hunters also shot animals with bows and arrows. They speared fish with long, sharpened poles, called **spears**, or trapped them in nets of woven plant fibers.

Men made all their weapons by hand, using materials such as stone, bone, wood, and feathers. They taught their sons about the various materials and how to work with them.

Thankful for the animals

The Anishinabe believed that all things were connected in the Sacred Circle of Life. Before each hunting and fishing trip, people offered prayers to the animals and asked them to sacrifice their lives for the hunter's family. When the hunter returned with an animal, his family offered thanks to it for giving up its life. The family also thanked the Creator for the hunter's skill. No one used any part of the animal until they had given thanks.

Keeping the balance

The Anishinabe respected animals and the balance of the natural world, so they killed only what they needed. They never fished or hunted an animal during its **mating season**. When they caught an animal, they were careful never to waste any part of it. They ate the animal's meat, used the bones to make tools, and made clothing, shoes, bedding, and wigwam coverings from its hide. They used other parts to make thread or medicines.

People spearfished year-round.

Food from the land

Foods that grew in fields and forests were important parts of the Anishinabe diet, especially in summer and autumn when many trees and plants grew fruits, seeds, and berries. Women and children searched the forests for cherries, blackberries, raspberries, blueberries, and strawberries.

Besides berries and other fruits, they also gathered herbs such as mint, which they used to make tea and to season foods. Some women also planted small gardens with pumpkins, corn, squash, potatoes, and beans. People ate some of the foods fresh and dried the rest for winter.

*The Anishinabe called wild rice **manoomin**, or "holy seed," in honor of the Creator. On the first night of the harvest, they prepared a huge feast and sang, danced, and prayed to give thanks.*

Wild rice

Wild rice was one of the Anishinabe's most important foods. It was not actually rice but a type of grain that grew on tall stalks of grass. It became ripe in late summer and early autumn. Families spent about six weeks harvesting, cleaning, and drying the wild rice.

To gather the rice grains, two people worked together in a canoe. One steered while the other pulled stalks over the canoe and knocked off the grains. When their canoe was full, the people took the rice ashore to clean and prepare it for use. First, the rice was **parched**, or heated over a fire to dry. The heat loosened its **husks**, or cases. Once the husks were loose, the grains had to be **jigged**. A man danced on them to finish rubbing off the husks. Women then put the rice in shallow trays and tossed it into the air so the husks would blow away. Finally, they sun-dried the rice so that it could be stored.

Maple sugar

People used maple sugar and syrup to add flavor to foods. They ate it with fruits, vegetables, meat, and fish. Sugar not only added flavor, but it also kept foods from spoiling.

Sugaring season

In the late winter, the Anishinabe began watching for crows—the first sign of spring. When the birds appeared, families moved to the bush to begin collecting sap and making maple syrup and sugar. Each family had its own **sugar bush**, or group of maple trees, to which it returned each year. To get the sap out of the trees, people cut notches into the trunks and hammered in sharp wooden spouts. Sap dripped out of the spouts into birchbark buckets.

Boiling it down

Women made sap into syrup and sugar by heating it. They put the sap into hide or birchbark containers and dropped hot rocks into it until it boiled. The longer the sap cooked, the thicker it became. When the sap was a smooth syrup, women put some of it into containers for storing. They boiled the rest until it became as thick as glue. The women then spooned it into wooden troughs and worked it with paddles until it cooled and formed sugar. For fun, they spooned some of the syrup onto the snow or into wooden molds, where it cooled into maple candy for the children.

People had to collect a lot of sap—it took almost 40 gallons (151 l) to make just one gallon (3.8 l) of syrup or three quarts (3.3 l) of maple sugar!

Clothing

Women made and decorated all the clothing their families wore. They made the clothing from soft animal hides and fur and used animal sinews to stitch the garments together. Women and girls decorated the finished items with porcupine quills and beads made of shell, bone, or stone.

Men's and boys' clothing

In warm weather, men wore breechcloths. Breechcloths were long strips of soft animal hide that were placed between the legs and then pulled up and under a belt so the edges hung over in the front and back. In cool weather, men added thigh-high leggings, which were pant-legs with loops that attached to a belt. Leggings were made of soft deer, elk, or moose hide. Men also wore fringed hide shirts. Boys dressed in similar clothing to that worn by men.

Women's and girls' clothing

Anishinabe women wore long hide dresses year-round. The dresses were stitched only at the shoulders. Women pulled the garments over their heads and then secured them with belts around their waists. The dresses had detachable sleeves, which women removed in warm weather. Beneath their dresses, women wore undergarments made of woven tree-bark fibers. When it was cooler, they added hide leggings that reached down to their knees. Girls wore clothing like that worn by women.

Headwear

Both men and women wore their hair long. Women usually pulled theirs into a low ponytail. For special occasions, they divided their hair into two braids near their ears. Most men wore their hair loose or in two braids. For special occasions or for battle, some men wore headpieces, called **roaches**, down the center of their heads. Roaches were made of deer fur or porcupine quills. In cool weather, people often wore fur caps, below left, or wrapped strips of deer skin around their heads.

Regalia

Besides their everyday clothing, the Anishinabe wore and carried special belts, bags, weapons, and tools, known as **regalia**. These items were made of wood, shells, feathers, horns, bone, and other natural materials. People made regalia for themselves or received regalia items as special gifts when they did good deeds or behaved bravely.

Women often dyed porcupine quills (left) and used them to create patterns such as those on the moccasins below.

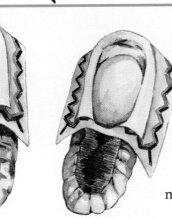

Soft, sturdy footwear

On their feet, the Anishinabe wore **moccasins**, which were soft shoes made from animal hide. They usually made their moccasins from moose hide, which was very durable, but they also made soft deer-hide moccasins for special occasions. Some historians believe the name "Ojibwe," which means "puckered," came from a description of the people's moccasins, which had puckered seams on top.

Fun and games

People had a lot of work to do, but they always made time for fun, too. Even after gathering food or working on other tasks all day, they often danced and sang together in the evenings. They also played many kinds of outdoor games and sports, including wrestling and running races. In the winter, when the weather was cold and damp, families spent happy hours inside their warm wigwams, playing games and telling stories. According to oral tradition, the story-telling season started with the first snowfall and ended with the first sound of thunder in spring.

One of the most popular outdoor sports was the one that people now call **lacrosse**. For fun, families and friends formed two teams, each of which had six to ten players. Neighboring groups and nations often used lacrosse games to settle disputes. In these games, teams were made up of hundreds or even thousands of people. Lacrosse was often part of spiritual ceremonies, as well. It was played with a small ball and long sticks that usually had a circular net or basket at one end. Using the sticks to catch, hold, and throw the ball, the players tried to score points by moving it across a goal line.

Children's sports and games

Children enjoyed all kinds of games. They played follow-the-leader, a version of hide-and-seek, and many other games that are still played today. They also competed in racing, wrestling, and various other sports. Handmade dolls were popular toys for girls, whereas boys often played with small bows and arrows.

Snowsnake

Shu-shu-may, or "snowsnake," was a popular winter game. The "snake" was a long wooden pole with a pointed end. Competitors slid their "snakes" across the snow or ice to see whose went the farthest.

Celebrations

When a major task was completed, people had good reason to sing, dance, and enjoy a feast. People also celebrated when they gathered at summer camps after a long winter separation. Men sometimes sat in a circle around large drums and sang together while women danced around them. Men and women also used smaller hand-held drums to accompany their songs. Everyone learned the traditional songs and dances when they were children, and they enjoyed performing them together. People sang and danced, not only for enjoyment, but also as part of spiritual ceremonies.

Beliefs and gratitude

Spirituality was an important part of life for the Anishinabe. They believed that all things came from the Creator and were linked in the Sacred Circle of Life. People respected everything around them, believing that they were connected to all living things. Every day, they offered thanks for the gifts they received from nature. They did so with prayers, songs, dances, and offerings to the Creator and the manitous that helped them.

Part of the Circle

The Anishinabe did not see themselves as separate from the Earth, and they always used natural things with the **seventh generation** in mind. They considered the effects their actions would have on the seventh generation of people after themselves. Thinking of the future and their effect on it helped ensure that the Anishinabe lived in balance and harmony with nature.

This painting, by Anishinabe artist Lois Beardslee, illustrates the story of Awasassi. Among other lessons, the story teaches that all creatures—no matter how big or small—have an important place in nature.

Sacred plants

The Anishinabe considered four plants to be sacred: tobacco, sage, sweetgrass, and cedar. People often burned these plants and used the smoke, called a **smudge**, to make themselves, a place, or an object pure. People also used tobacco as an offering when they prayed and thanked the Creator. Sometimes they burned it, so that the smoke would carry their messages to the Creator. Other times, they left tobacco in sacred places. People carried their tobacco in special bags such as the one shown right.

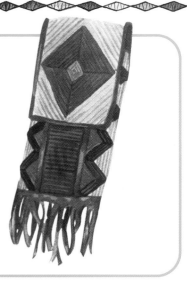

The Midewiwin

For thousands of years, the Anishinabe recorded their history and beliefs on birchbark scrolls such as the one shown above. A group of people, called the **Midewiwin**, protected the scrolls. Members of the Midewiwin knew a great deal about using herbs and plants to treat sickness, and they often led special ceremonies. Their knowledge and teachings were known as **Mide**.

Dreams and dreamcatchers

Dreams were important to the Anishinabe. Their word for dream, *bawedjigewin*, also means "vision." The Anishinabe believed that dreams were a connection to the spirit world and contained important messages. Some dreams even foretold the future. People paid close attention to their dreams and interpreted them carefully. Children were encouraged to remember their dreams and were taught what different images and symbols in dreams meant. Some Anishinabe made **dreamcatchers** such as the one shown below right. A dreamcatcher was made of a round bent-twig frame, with a web of sinew in its center. A hole in the middle of the web allowed good dreams to pass through to the dreamer. Bad dreams got tangled up in the web, and at the first light of day, the sun burned them up.

Contact with the Europeans

The arrival of Europeans in North America in the early 1600s changed the lives of all Native peoples, including the Anishinabe. Europeans brought with them many sicknesses to which the Anishinabe had never been exposed. Thousands of Anishinabe died of illnesses such as smallpox, measles, cholera, and tuberculosis. The Europeans saw the world differently than Native people did, which also caused problems for the Anishinabe. Europeans believed that animals and trees should be used for profit and that land should be owned privately. Many also believed that Native peoples were "savages" whom they either had to conquer or convert to European ways.

French fur traders were the first to arrive in Anishinabe territories. They quickly realized that the Anishinabe were expert trappers with far better skills than their own. They began trading with the Anishinabe for otter, fox, mink, wolf, bear, and beaver furs. They offered guns, beads, woven cloth, wool blankets, and metal items such as fish hooks, knives, and needles, in exchange for the furs. Some Anishinabe began changing the way they hunted, no longer taking only what they needed for their families. European trappers often hunted animals until they disappeared from an area, leaving the Anishinabe with very little game to hunt for themselves and their families.

Conflicts arise

By the end of the 1600s, beavers and other animals were scarce in many areas. People from several nations, including the Anishinabe, began moving from their traditional territories in search of animals. Many northern Anishinabe remained in their territories, but others spread farther into present-day Wisconsin, Minnesota, and Ontario. When nations moved into the territories of others, conflicts often arose with the people already living and hunting there. During the 1700s, France and England began fighting over the fur trade. Many Great Lakes nations were drawn into the battle. Most sided with the French, who were less interested in settling on their land than the British were.

Forced changes

By the late 1700s, England defeated France. South of the Great Lakes, the United States was formed. The Great Lakes area was controlled by the British and American governments, which did not recognize Native territories. Both wanted Native lands, and they tricked or forced some nations into giving them up. The Anishinabe, however, were able to keep some of their lands through skilled **diplomacy**. Both governments tried to "civilize" the Anishinabe by forcing them to adopt European lifestyles. They sent Anishinabe children to boarding schools where they were allowed to speak only English. Non-natives tried to make Native people feel ashamed of their cultures.

The people today

Today, thousands of Anishinabe live in the United States and Canada. They are known by many names, including Ojibwe, Saulteaux, Mississauga, and Chippewa. They are proud of their heritage, and many are working to preserve their language, traditions, and beliefs. Some still gather maple sugar and wild rice in the traditional ways. You can learn more about the Anishinabe's past and present on the Internet. Try these sites:

- www.millelacsojibwe.org
- www.saulttribe.org/teachings.htm
- www.nativetech.org/shinob/index.html

Glossary

Note: Boldfaced words that are defined in the book may not appear in the glossary.

Algonquian A group of related Native languages spoken by the majority of nations in the western Great Lakes region

alliance An association of two or more Native groups for the purpose of a common goal

camp A group of people living in portable dwellings; a village made up of such dwellings

clan A group of people who share an animal spirit as their ancestor

council A group of people called together to give advice, discuss a problem, or make a decision

diplomacy Skill in dealing with people and negotiating agreements

elder An older, respected member of a family, group, or nation

fast To eat little or no food or to avoid eating certain kinds of food

generation A step or level in a family, such as the children, the parents, or the grandparents

indigenous Describing people or things that are native to, or born in, a specific area

manitou A spirit or power that is present in all things in nature

mating season The time of year during which animals produce offspring

nation A large group of people who share common customs, origins, history, and language

oral tradition The stories that are told, from one generation to the next, about a group of people and its history

preserve To treat or store food in a way that stops it from spoiling

scroll A rolled sheet of birch bark, especially one with writing on it

snare A trap consisting of a loop of rope that tightens around birds and small animals

sinew The strong connective tissue of animals, dried for use as string or thread

territory An area of land and water on which a group of people traditionally lived, hunted, fished, and gathered food

tipi A portable dwelling that has a cone-shaped framework of poles covered with animal skins or bark

vision A dream experience that foretells the future or results in a deeper understanding of life

wild rice The edible grain of a tall grass that grows in swampy areas bordering lakes or rivers

Index

1 2 3 4 5 6 7 8 9 0   Printed in the U.S.A.   2 1 0 9 8 7 6 5 4 3